101 Ways to Tell Your Child "I Love You"

Vicki Lansky

illustrations by Kaye White

BP
BOOK PEDDLERS

Thanks to Abby Rabinovitz for all her help in getting this book to print.

Creative through print by Pettit Network, Inc.
Cover design by Travis Fortner

ISBN 13: 978-1-931863-51-3

Lansky, Vicki
  101 ways to tell your child "I love you."

  1. Parenting—Miscellanea. 2. Love, Maternal.
3. Love, Paternal. I. Title. II. Title: One hundred
one ways to tell your child " I love you." III. Title:
One hundred and one ways to tell your child "I love
you."
HQ755.8.L354   2008   649'.1   88-20345

BOOK PEDDLERS, 2828 HEDBERG DRIVE, MINNETONKA, MN 55305
952-544-1154 • www.bookpeddlers.com

printed in China

1 2 3 4 5 6 7 8 9 10 • 15 14 13 12 11 10 09

Dedication

to my three very dear granddaughters

Sienna Cecilia Lansky
India Cecilia Lansky
Belize Cecilia Lansky

...and their terrific parents, Doug and Signe,
who are quite wonderful at letting
their children know they are loved

Introduction

    Although it's an obvious thought, I was surprised to learn from an incident with my young daughter that using the words I love you to express "I love you" wasn't always enough. She had been a bit low for a day or two, and while the "I love you's" and hugs were there for her, they didn't seem to lift the cloud that hung over her.

    After one particularly pleasant day, I told her when I tucked her in that night how much I had enjoyed her that day.

For many days afterward she would ask me, "Are you enjoying me?" Fortunately, I could answer YES! It was like flipping a light switch inside her.

There are so many ways to let your children know you love them. Love is shown with affection, laughter, in private times together, in hugs and kisses and in 101 other ways, such as you'll find in this book.

You may not wish to use all of these wonderful ideas, as they will not all be comfortable for you or appropriate for your child's age. But I do think you'll find many new and special ways to tell your child, "I love you."

Have a terrific time with those you use...and come up with on your own!

Vicki Lansky

Have a secret I LOVE YOU signal, maybe three squeezes of a hand, a V-sign with your fingers, or touching your nose and then your child's nose.

Spontanous gestures let your child know the fun side of love. Dad, stop in the middle of shaving to give a surprise shaving-cream kiss to your watching child. . .

or stop in the middle of a bedtime story to give a big I LOVE YOU hug and kiss — just because you couldn't resist doing it!

Make up a simple love song with your own words to an old familiar tune, such as this one to the tune of "Frère Jacques":

"I love Indie, I love Indie
She's a dear, she's a dear
What a lovely daughter,
What a lovely daughter!
Glad she's here, glad she's here!"

Learn to say I LOVE YOU in sign language.

Share a special verse to let your child understand just how wonderful he or she is to you.

Make up a photo album of your child for him or her to keep (kids love to look back on the "old days") or a scrapbook of first drawings and other precious memorabilia. Or help your child produce a ME book, complete with old and new photos, a list of hobbies, interests, toys and pets.

♡

Leave a small surprise gift, such as stickers or a new marker, in an odd or unexpected place — in a pocket, a lunch box or even in the refrigerator.

When asked "What for?" answer, "Because I love you and I wanted to do something special for you."

Lie outside on a blanket with your child on a fine summer night and watch for shooting stars.

Look steadily into your child's eyes, smile but don't say a word, for a few moments.

There is no more loving gift than listening. Listen not only with your ears but with your eyes.

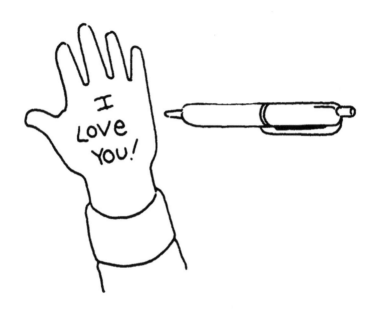

Draw a heart and the words I LOVE YOU on the back of your child's hand with a ballpoint pen. It's both naughty and nice!

Come up with a new anagram for your child's initials. For instance, Adrienne Gail Smith's initials might stand for <u>A</u>lways <u>G</u>iving <u>S</u>unshine or Sky Allan Lewis could be:

<u>S</u> ings
<u>A</u> bout
<u>L</u> ove

Create an annual day for your child ('Doug's Day,' for example) on which your child has special privileges such as being the last to go to bed, answering the phone, or pushing the elevator button. This makes a nice half-birthday celebration.

♡

Plant a kiss on your child's palm and roll his or her fingers tightly to "hold" it safely for later use or whenever it is needed.

Buy or make personalized gifts: anything with your child's name on it makes it special...

from personalized barrettes and special-ordered pencils to iron-on letters on jeans or back packs.

Leave heart drawings or love messages or "with love from..." notes in unusual places such as on the bathroom mirror, the front door, on cereal boxes...even on shoes or boots.

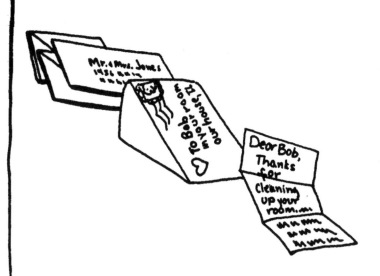

Mail a letter or card to your child, even if you haven't gone away. Getting mail is a special event for all children but especially so at holiday times or when they are sick.

♡

Decorate a paper or vinyl placemat with something personalized like "Eating Spot of the Best Four-Year-Old in the Whole World."

Take a video clip of your child as "the star."
Singing, dancing, and playing sports all make
good center-stage performances. Send it to the
grandparents online but probably best <u>not</u> to
post it on the Internet.

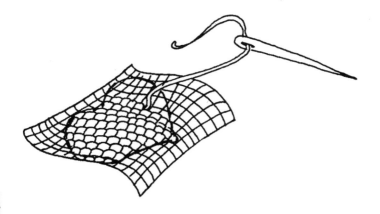

If you enjoy a needlecraft or woodworking, make your child a special present, such as a heart with his or her initials.

Make a "monogram garden" outside. In your yard, plant blossoming annuals of the same color in the shape of your child's name or initials.

Indoors you can sprout seeds on a large, flat sponge floating on a shallow dish of water.

Create bedtime stories in which your child is the hero or heroine in an adventure story. Or if you are reading aloud from a favorite book, change the name of the main character to that of your child.

Let your child hear you praise him or her to others. Kids love to hear good things about themselves, especially when they 'accidentally' overhear you.

Hang one or more red paper hearts by a string or ribbon in your child's doorway for him or her to walk through as a good-morning surprise or when getting up from a nap.

Say to your child, "I'm so glad you were given to me!"

Along with a good-night kiss, tell your child you appreciated all the good things he or she did that day, such as picking up toys, helping with the laundry, or making you laugh.

♡

Write a loving message on an inflated balloon for your child to find in an unexpected place such as in a drawer or under the bedcovers. Filling a whole closet with balloons is even more memorable!

Create a "Welcome Home" or "I Love You" banner on a roll of shelf paper as a surprise after the first day of school.

Serve your child's dinner on a special plate — perhaps a good china dish or a favorite one you keep on display — to celebrate a triumph or act as a reminder on a bad day that he or she is always very important to you.

Leave praising announcements such as "I love Leslie's smile" on your refrigerator, kitchen chalkboard, or other family message center, for all to see. You can also post report cards and other special 'awards' in the same places.

Spend time online with your child. Just like it is good to read aloud to a child who can already read, even a computer savvy child, enjoys time together online. Play games, create a screensaver with your child's photo or create 'I Love You' cards for family and friends as well as each other!

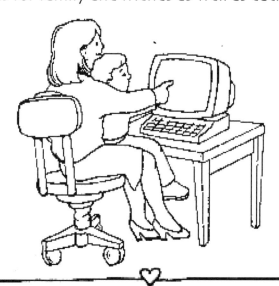

Make an outing to the hospital where your child was born and talk about his or her 'birth' day. Stop at the nursery during visiting hours to see the new babies, and maybe stop at the cafeteria for a bite to eat.

♡

Create your own series of signs to put by the driveway or posted down a hallway.

NO MATTER WHAT

YOU SAY OR DO

REMEMBER ALWAYS

I LOVE YOU

LOVE,
    MOM/DAD

"I like the way you..." is a loving message for a child to hear, appropriate for anything from thumb wrestling to brushing hair to making a drawing.

Ask your child to pick a
number from 1 to 10.
Then deliver that many kisses!

Pick a nickname for your child that will enhance his or her self-image. "Sara Sharer," for example, "Darnell the Dancer," or "Josh the Joyful."

Let your child crawl into bed with you in the morning for a snuggle if last night's bedtime hug was missed . . . or even if it wasn't!

♡

Let your children know that they are — and will be — loveable at every age. Tell a 5-year-old, "I'm going to love you when you are 6 years old . . . when you are 16 years old . . .

when you are 26 years old . . . and even when you are 60 years old." Or simply say, " . . . and when you're all grown-up!"

Lay out a secret treasure hunt for your child with a map or a series of clues that will lead from one room to the next. The treasure is an I LOVE YOU message and a surprise such as a book, toy or IOU for a trip to a pet store or zoo.

Say "I love you" in pig Latin:

"I-ya ov-lay ou-yay!"

A delightful verbal game that you can make one of your family traditions is the following:

Parent :
"Have I told you how much I love you today?"

Child:
"No."

Parent:
"I love, you, I love you, I love you."
(smooch, smooch, smooch)

With a lipstick or eyeliner, write a love message or draw a heart on the bathroom mirror as a morning surprise for your children to see when they are brushing their teeth.

Play "I love your more than . . .". You can be-
gin with "I love you more than all the leaves on
the trees," and then move on to ". . .all the ice
cream in the world, . . .stars in the sky," and so
on. Let your   children come
up with some   of their own.

There are two sides of love.

One is giving, the other is receiving.

Children sometimes show us their love when we're busy or angry, but we need to let them show it when they want to.

After all, that is how we do it.

Let a hand puppet or stuffed animal talk for you, telling your child how much you love him or her, and nuzzling up to dispense kisses.

Children with brothers and sisters don't always understand that there is enough of their parents' love to go around. Using candles, you can show how your love can be shared without

being diminished. Light one candle to represent Mom, and another for Dad. Then light one for each child. Remark how each flame is as bright as the others. This is how love works.

Do you have an "I Love You Up to Here" chart? It's a great way to mark your child's height periodically, on a door frame or a large piece of poster board.

Wake your child up with a kiss. What nicer or
more loving way to start a day?

Write "I love (your child's name)" with chalk on a sidewalk, driveway, or porch as a public display of affection.

Let your children know how special it is to be their parent by saying, " I love being your mom," "I love being your dad," or "I love you for making my life wonderful."

Make a heart-shaped I LOVE YOU puzzle.
On a piece of cardboard, write your message
(such as "I love you 2 pieces"), then cut it up so
your child can put it back together.

♡

Take your child on a secret destination car ride, maybe even blindfolding him or her until you are there. "There" can be an ice cream stop, a favorite scenic place, or a playground or park.

Write I LOVE YOU on a ball and play catch with it. With every toss, your child will be "catching" a bit of love from you.

Create a big family-group hug as one of your traditions where everyone huddles together and shares hugs and kisses.

See how many words you and your child can
make from the letters I L-O-V-E Y-O-U.

Make an I LOVE YOU heart-shaped cake from a square cake and a round one.

Step #1

Step #2

Step #3

Make a verbal "love list" of your child's face:
"I love your nose . . . your ears . . . your eyes"
— and plant a kiss on each.

Go for a walk in a new winter snow, in the moonlight, or in a warm summer rain, for a memorable event. In fresh snow, stomp your child's name or make heart shape designs.

Put your ear to your child's belly button, saying that you are listening to a little voice in there. After a moment, announce, "I hear a request for a hug." Then comply!

Take turns in this little rhyming game:

I Love You..........Yes, I do!
I Love You..........Wouldn't you?
I Love You..........I'd wear your shoe.
I Love You..........Kiss me, too.

See how many you and your child can make up!

Look up the word LOVE in the dictionary to-gether. Then remind your child that that's how you feel about him or her.

Love (lŭv) *n.* *1.* An intense feeling....

♡

Create a LOVE collage of your child's name,
initials, and personal interests. Cut out words,
letters, and pictures from magazines or news-
papers to spell out your message, and glue
them on a posterboard or foamcore board.

♥

If you leave the house before your kids get up in the morning, leave a love note under each glass of breakfast juice you've poured for them.

♥LOVE LICENSE♥

NAME _____ (EYES)

is licensed to love and be loved!

ADDRESS _____ (AGE)

CITY/STATE _____

X _____
        SIGNATURE
VALID FOREVER AND EVER AND EVER!

Make up a "Love License" on an index card or design one on your computer. First design and make one for your child, and then help that child make one for each member of the family.

After disciplining your child, an important loving message is, "I don't always like your behavior, but I always love you."

Give your children framed family pictures for their bedrooms. Be sure to date it and sign the photo with "love."

Give "Eskimo" kisses by rubbing noses! Or an "angel's kiss" by kissing a child's shut eyelids!

Going out for the evening? Try some pillow talk. Write a love note and leave it on your child's pillow for him or her to read at bedtime. (For a younger child, a sitter can read it.)

If your child is old enough, encourage a response on your pillow to welcome you home. (Don't forget to use the universal code for hugs and kisses.... **OOXXOOXX!**)

When was the last time you gave a bear hug?
No matter what the child's age, a caring,
crushing hug is memorable. Try to be the last
one to let go — you will leave behind a
wonderful feeling.

Create fancy-named kisses to trade with your child, such as a "double chocolate chip," a "whipped cream mocha," or maybe an "orange meringue" kiss. Especially luscious at bedtime!

♡

When you travel, try to bring home a small gift—free or otherwise: even a hotel note pad and pen, or a postcard set from the city you've visited. It's a great way to say, "I really thought of you when I was gone."

Here's a "knock, knock" joke that delights!

Knock, Knock
Who's there?

Olive

Olive who?
Olive you.

♡

Sing songs to your child that speak of love such as, "I Love You a Bushel and A Peck," "All You Need is Love," "Our Love is Here to Stay," "Baby Love," "What the World Needs Now is Love Sweet Love," and "The Glory of Love," to name a few.

Hang mistletoe even when the holidays end to assure a constant supply of kisses.

Bring home the gift of a fresh flower
for your child, or even
a whole bouquet!

♡

Out of stiff board,
(and maybe using your
computer) make large
'coins' with

GOOD FOR A HUG

GOOD FOR A KISS

printed on them.

Redeem as needed!

Draw the letters I L-O-V-E Y-O-U on your child's back with your finger during a bedtime backrub.

Send a secret I LOVE YOU message that must be turned toward a mirror to be read, or decoded with a secret code.

Decorate a little bag of loving surprises and
put it near your child's bed to be found in
the morning. You might include a little chalkboard, a small book, or maybe even a piece of
fruit.

Make LOVE ME cracker snacks. On a round cracker, put a cheese spread, olive slices for eyes, half a grape for a nose and dried red cranberries for a smiley mouth.

Let your children know that distance doesn't lessen love. When you travel, tell them you think of them when you're up in the plane flying through the clouds. Also, let them know that their relatives who live far away away love them and think of them often.

In how many languages can you say
"I love you"?

I Love You:	*Language:*	*sounds like:*
je t'aime	French	je tem
te amo	Spanish	tay ahmo
ich liebe dich	German	ick leebe dick
lo tiamo	Italian	yo teeahmo
jag älskar dig	Swedish	yagh alskawr day

Make hamburgers special by "decorating" them with a 'heart' using ketchup from a squeeze bottle.

Label a jar "Hugs and Kisses," and fill it with slips of paper that say "I need a hug," "I need a kiss," and "I need both a hug and a kiss." Then let your children select one every day. Perhaps put this jar next to their bed.

Teach your child how to make pretty paper hearts, using folded colored paper or tracing heart-shaped cookie cutters.

Make a pennant or a flag for your child's wall from a piece of paper or felt, and decorate it

with his or her name or initials, the words *I love you*, and plenty of hearts.

A surprise breakfast in bed will make the day really special.

Fill a large jar with nuts, add a ribbon to make it festive, and attach a note that says, "I'm nuts about you."

When grocery shopping, let your child share in some of the food decisions for the dinner meal— especially dessert!

BOO BOO'S MENU

How many ways are there to say
"You're great!"?

There is nothing like cuddling up with kids and a good book to show them how much you love them, as well as how much fun it is to read.

♡

Make an alphabet cereal message. Spell out
I LOVE YOU
on top of toast or on your child's plate.

Write a secret message-in-pictures.

Or disguise a message with this code that children love to use: A=1; B=2; C=3; etc.

For a shortcut:

9/12-15-22-5/25-15-21
I L O V E   Y O U

Come up behind your child, put your hands over his or her eyes, and say:

"Somebody loves you
Who could it be?

Now you see,
The one who loves you is me."

Pluck daisy petals for
"I love you, I love you not."

(Be sure to end up
with "I love you"!)

Just once, place a freshly lipsticked smooch on your child's cheek, forehead, or hand to "show" your love.

Have a discussion about the color of love. Ask your child what color love is, and why.

How many "red" things can you name together? There are apples, hearts, balloons, markers, ketchup bottles, and...

Use the letters in your child's name to create a personal note or a colorful poster. Or at a crafts store pick small wooden letters for your child's name or initials. Paint and glue to a box or heart-shape form as a special keepsake.

S   is for Special
I   is for Intelligent
E   is for Energetic
N   is for Nice
N   is for Nifty
A   is for Affectionate

Make your own dot-to-dot heart-shapes for your child to connect. Even make dot-to-dots for the letters in 'I love you.'

There is nothing more loving than something from the oven. Spend quality cooking or baking time with your child. Shape a home-made pizza as a heart. Heart-shaped cookie cutters have a multitude of uses from cutting cheese slices to pancakes as well as sandwiches.

Make up I LOVE YOU coupons to give as a gift . . . just because "I love you." These can be for anything: a back rub, watching a movie, playing a favorite board game, or a trip to a playground. Make up your own and use those at the back of this book.

Make sure you have a signed, legal will appointing a guardian and an executor regardless of the size of your estate. (They can be the same or different.) This is truly the most loving and thoughtful gift you can give your children.

LOVE COUPON

GOOD FOR:

_____

LOVE COUPON

GOOD FOR:

_____

LOVE COUPON

GOOD FOR:

_____

For more information about all my books,
please visit my website at:
www.practicalparenting.com

To purchase additional copies of this
or any of my other titles call 952-544-1154.
A free catalog is also available.

Vicki Lansky
Book Peddlers/Practical Parenting
2828 Hedberg Drive
Minnetonka, MN 55305
vlansky@bookpeddlers.com